The Prayer

A Collection of Poems

Anuja Anand

Bigfoot Publications

Because, there's a writer in everyone.

The Prayer : A Collection of Poems
Author: Anuja Anand

First Published by
Bigfoot06 Publications (OPC) Pvt. Ltd.
1st floor, BSR Building near Vishal Mega Mart,
Daultabad Flyover, Laxman Vihar Phase 3,
Gurugram, Haryana (122001)
Website: www.bigfootpublications.in
Email: info@bigfootpublications.in

First Edition: March, 2024

ISBN Print Book - **978-81-970448-4-7**

Typeset in Garamond 12pt
by Yachika Prajapati For Bigfoot06 Publications

Printed in India

Introduction

books have always understood me like no one else; they have been my best companions. when i stumble upon a phrase that resonates deeply, i pause, embracing the book, pulling it closer to my chest.

with the same intention of providing comfort to readers, i have penned this book.
it's a reassurance that you are seen, understood, and never alone.

as a survivor.
the trauma whispered subtly yet persistently that life was not worth living.

as a warrior.
amidst the turmoil, my writing remained a constant.
i poured out my pain, my joy, my emptiness onto the pages, hoping to find my inner voice.

as a believer.
each poem and quote within these pages is a testament to my yearning for solace.

"the prayer" embodies both comfort and lamentation. it is a surrender to the overwhelming pain, a dialogue between self and the sacred, and healing through prayerful reflection.

it's a cry about the unexplainable
a union of hearts that grieve
it's a confinement in the reliable
a fable of contemporary weave

it's laying in the arms of a lover
an offering of both comfort and complaint
it's a canvas painted with life's color
a gentle caress that relieves the pain

it's recollection of the lost time
a zeal to keep you closer
it's your ache that is mine
a quest for love that is over

it's relinquishing myself to you
a hope that our hearts beat in unison
it's love that's pure and true
a faith in both self and the season

~the prayer

"Courage is fear that has said its prayers."

- Dorothy Bernard

"Unapologetically honest, Anuja's writing puts the power back into the hands from which it was stolen"

- Ann Harikeertan (Writer, Editor, Doctor)

"It is a beautiful literary work that can be incorporated for the purpose of critical appreciation and education"

- Mehfisha Anjum (Writer, Professor, Psychologist)

"Her writings remind me of a strong, powerful force not to be reckoned with, yet so gentle, safe, and inviting at the same time."

- Niru Ramasamy (Writer, Artist, Social Worker)

Acknowledgments

i am deeply grateful to all those who have guided me with love and patience throughout my journey. first and foremost, i want to express my heartfelt thanks to my cousin, Sakshi Anand, whose unwavering support has been a constant source of strength for me. i am also indebted to my mother, Mradul Srivastava, whose own passion for writing ignited the flame of creativity within me.

to my mentor and therapist, Mehfisha Anjum, i owe an immense debt of gratitude. your guidance has helped me navigate through the darkness and fears that once engulfed me. your teachings on unconditional love have been transformative, marking a pivotal moment in my journey towards healing. this book would not have been possible without you.

my grandfather, R.N. Srivastava always harbored the dream of getting published, yet he never could. so, i am deeply grateful for the opportunity to aspire to fulfill his dream by publishing my own work.

i extend my sincere appreciation to my friends, Deepansh and Ann, whose understanding and encouragement have provided me with a safe space for expression and growth.

to the readers who have embarked on this journey with me, i offer my heartfelt thanks. your willingness to explore the depths of these verses is a gift beyond measure. it is your curiosity and openness that breathe life into this book.

i would like to express my heartfelt gratitude to my friend Adya Prabha, whose belief in my writings has been a constant source of inspiration. even though she is no longer with us, i have tried to keep her wisdom and encouragement alive through my verses, a few of which were edited by her.

Dedications

to my dad who made me who i am today

to those who are hiding away with broken, messy, and unloved parts of themselves, hesitant and ashamed, let my words be a gentle embrace

in loving memory of Adya Prabha (1997-2020)

The Contents

Bonus Sections

Poems of Adoration

in a world where my anxieties stink
you were the calming scent of lavenders

i prayed for those who did me wrong
i prayed for those who inflicted harm on me
i prayed for solace from your afflictions

i know no other way of letting go

all this time, i believed i was the author of this book
yet, it seems the book was crafting itself through me

it needed to emerge from a womb liberated from
fears, doubts, shame, and guilt

twice i nearly birthed it – once in 2021 and again in 2022, but i
wasn't prepared to embrace motherhood just yet. as the
delivery date approached, discomfort escalated into
excruciating pain –

i had to break myself open for creation to unfold
this time, i vowed not to let it perish before it could take its
first breath
i refused to stifle its existence before it could flourish
love surged through my veins, signaling it was time

my water broke and the words sprang to life

~ creation

prayer is a form of praise—the highest expression of love.

i understand you're not perfect,
but to me, you are.

watch my selfless serenade
as i sing to the soaring sparrow
with the sun tied in my twin braid
i danced naked in your afterglow

grief bestowed me with grace
i kept weeping for my estranged soul
losing myself in your euphoric embrace
only to find that you're the path and the goal

challenging them servitude
i devoured the forbidden fruit
it's my flaws and my fortitude
rising from and returning to the root

my absolute surrender
i will go wherever you take me
now that my eyes are open
you have finally made me see

watch my selfless serenade
as i sing to the downy dove
with the moon tied in my twin braid
i danced naked in your love

i whispered to my body
as i let my tears wash off the stains

"you can never be impure!
you are the earth, right after the rains"

They pushed me aside in a corner
made me stand at the back of the stage
i smiled through every day of the torture
letting their opinions confine me into a cage

i blamed the melanin in my skin
i blamed the lengths of my bone
i blamed the flab beneath my chin
i blamed the sincerity of my tone

my fingers got twisted around six strings
childish were my melancholic rhyme
is this why they chopped off the angels' wings?
like how I was made to feel unworthy of what's mine

i believed every word they said
as i let them impregnated me with self-doubt
conveniently, they called me mad
without knowing what i am really about

i tasted freedom on my lips
dripping like flowers from a tree
their voices have loosened the grip
and love decided to set me free

"i don't understand your idea
of perfect love," he said
"your world of poetry is woven
with a melancholic thread"

"i don't know how to
settle for less," i said
"love sounds like a great idea
but only inside my head"

i looked at you with belief
but my rhymes don't seek affections
my idea of love is perfect
only when it has imperfections

"you will never understand
my idea of perfect love," i said
"my world of poetry is inked
with scars that never bled

for me, love is nothing
but a synonym of your name
and wondering why i let you mess
with the right side of my brain

i looked away with belief
that i will find you in all directions
my idea of love is perfect
only when it has imperfections

~the perfect love

i don't have your picture
but i know how to picture those
curious eyes, and that solemn look
i always end up drawing your eyes
on every page of my notebook

the artist in me loves
your leggy, lopsided body
masterpieces like you anyway
are beyond the line of symmetry

allow my fingers to trace constellations
for one last time, i would beg
from the mole on your chest to
the one on the back of your neck

allow me to hold your hand
for one last time, before you desist
i will not go further and stop painting
my universe on the mole on your wrist

the artist in me loves
your uncouth, ugly edges
masterpieces like you anyway
are worth keeping as sketches

~ the muse

i keep whirling in the wind
to be carried away in your arms
longing for you when the lights are dimmed
on the bed, naked and disarmed

will i ever be able to see your face?
they say you'll be the death of me
i will move in sync with your pace
with all my rivers falling into your sea

oh, my groom, with your arrow and bow
what do you look like?
sneaking in through the window
only to spend the night

i looked for you in all the corners
is it your shape on the edge of the bed?
hold me close and keep me warmer
making love to each other like a newlywed

this doubt made you go
what do you have to hide from me?
you left and asked me not to follow
oh, my love, return to your psyche

~ the doubt

you turned into a butterfly
visited me from the kingdom of the dead
soon the riverbeds will dry
as i will be holding you in our bed

i don't want to leave
they say you have held me captive
my mother is looking everywhere for me
but you left me here enchanted

so fragile, the keeper of the dead
longing for me to bless your soul
so delicate, the peck on my forehead
watch opposite weave a whole

i am the queen of the eternal spring
wistful winter followed by my farewell
i rule the underworld next to him
waiting beyond the rivers of hell

~ pomegranate seeds

i watch the angel's smile
a soft voice calls my name
this is an end to my exile
and a prelude to my pain

i lied a thousand times before
and truth took its time to reveal
love, you have always made me implore
now rupture my soul into dust to heal

your touch broke me down into tears
what did i do to deserve this?
i'll hold you with no favor and fears
to safely carry you through the abyss

i looked for treasure in all directions
sympathized with the shepherd's stupidity
i almost lost faith in the one
while all along it lived in me

i summoned you into my empty arms

only if i could borrow you tonight
i would give everything away to be with you
only to dance with you the whole night
and stare at you blending with the view

my arms around your neck
moving to the rhythm of our grief
your arms behind my back
dancing till we both can't breathe

the gentle breeze turned to a hurricane
as we danced with the farthest stars
i admit that i hate to let you go again
slipping away from my helpless arms

can i just pull you a little closer
and whisper everything i couldn't say?
i don't care if this world is over
now that i have stolen you away

i'll summon you into my empty arms

~ divine choreography

saw you looking at me across the hall
in your best suit with a red tie
the world so big, yet so small
saw me looking at you but didn't say a 'hi'

i noticed that you cut your hair
do you now feel like a new man?
like we are strangers in a familiar room
drawing up some escape plan

you speak so clear, so very gentle
crossing paths with you, boy
is never purely coincidental

and i will never be able to tell
what you taste like, boy
maybe some cigarettes
but i guess, mostly starlight

and your lips so soft, so very gentle
crossing paths with you, boy
is never purely coincidental

it was springtime
the season of butterflies and lovers
the smell of your cigarettes
linger as the sultry summers

we took the wrong train twice
tangled in earphones, listening to 'collide'
i didn't want you to see through me so
i chose the nook of your neck to hide

it was springtime
the season of drunken mistakes
the taste of our very first kiss
lingers as we snuck out for the coffee breaks

i traced those permanent scars
on your back that i scratched
we made love in a hotel room
with no strings attached

i found my religion
when i made love with you
you were my only sin
darling, you are my only virtue

~ beautiful crimes

i wish we can talk a bit longer
we can't deceive the sun, can we?
i wish i can stay a bit stronger
but as the morning comes, you'll have to leave

saying it only makes things tough
you know how much i hate 'i love yous'
but i swear to stare at you long enough
from the time you wake up till you tie your shoes

your sweat dripping on me
you ask me to look you in the eye
like the rivers flowing back to the sea
and 283 days long rain falling from the sky

it sometimes kills me to love you so
we can't deceive fate, can we?
and once again i will have to let you go
wish i left first than to watch you leave

a sunflower despising the sun
someone, please slow down the time
thousand words left unspoken
i can't watch you walking past the check-in line

i stayed up all night looking at your face
i hate the sun, the roads, and your suitcase
let me tell you there's one more thing i hate -
kissing you goodbye at the airport gate

~ the airport

Poems of Confessions

i looked out of my window
feeling like a goon
because the sky is clear
but it's still raining in my room

i can't hit the notes
so, i play the guitar till my fingers bled
i know why all the strings are mute
so, i sit naked on my bed

and will i ever be clean?
his touch covered me with grime
he made my existence obscene
stealing something that was once mine

there's no place to go
nowhere to hide
the plant that he stole

it died
it died

did your heart cry out loud seeking forgiveness
as mine did?

who am i
to not forgive?

knees sinking into her chest
and the arch of her curved spine
on the edge of the bed, she rests
hearing her mother's pertinent whine

her pain is not just as achy
who defined femininity for her?
sit like a lady, talk like a lady
who defined conformity for her?

your love ruptures my lung
it ties my gut into a knot
vengefully, it chops off my tongue
it makes me who i am not

she turned kind only to be cruel
and covered herself in veils of lies
she adorned silence as the finest jewel
churning the heaven between her thighs

it's been a couple of seasons
since you watched the sun rise
rather made friends with demons
showed up late and later improvised

smothering under the pile of delays
you wish for some extra time to borrow
lying around on your bed for a few days
you decided to leave it all for tomorrow

shall i tell you the colors in my fiction
how i silently sleepwalk into your daydream
are you a prey of their malediction
or a hostage of your fragile self-esteem?

smothering under the pile of shame
you keep on blaming it all on sorrow
burnt down the castle with a careless flame
that you thought you'd put out tomorrow

when did time turn into a foe?
you didn't even care to realize
rather made friends with demons
showed up late and later improvised

~ the procrastination

my guilt is a shapeshifter

it consumed me
and then turned into blame
that devoured others

my aunt welcomed a son on July 14th, and they named him 'Anuj', after me, which means "younger brother." looking into his innocent eyes, the overwhelming guilt consumed me.

his smile, reminiscent of my own innocence, tugged at my heartstrings.

the thought of the world's inevitable cruelty tightening my chest, i couldn't help but worry about the countless ways it would hurt him.

i longed to shield him from the pain, but i knew it was futile.

he's 5 now
and knows all the cheat codes to his favorite games.

~ cheat codes

i used to look forward to parent-teacher meetings, eager to
witness the joy on your face when you spotted my name
among the top rankers on the blackboard.

i willingly sacrificed myself, devoting tirelessly to every
endeavor in hopes of capturing that same radiance in your eyes.

in my determination to become your favored child, i even
found myself locked in silent competition with my own siblings.
but despite my efforts, i cannot recall the last time i saw you
genuinely proud of me.

and i can not recall the last time i felt truly worthy.

up until now, i have been seeking your permission to be myself;
but from this moment forward, i will simply be me.

~ the validation

the image of my mother tirelessly giving herself only to be taken for granted, is etched into my memory. as a homemaker, she never once took a day off from her duties, neglecting her own needs until she became a stranger to herself in the mirror.

witnessing her suffering, i vowed not to follow in her footsteps. i refused to endure until my body grew numb to abuse and my mind turned into a cloud of trauma.

i didn't want silence to be my voice.

when i look in the mirror now, all i see is her reflection, smiling back at me
the bruises left by the abuse have numbed my body, and the thunderstorms clouding my judgment feel familiar.

i speak with silence now.

~ comparable suffering

when i was 5, my mother taught me
how to color within the lines of an outlined artwork,
transforming my chaos into boundless creativity.

the secret to pristine art was blending colors
without crossing lines,
carefully filling the void spaces.

i am 25 now, my once vibrant palette
is marred by spilled colors
and the encroachment of others' filth.

the empty spaces that once patiently waited to be filled
are now tarnished,
rendering me an undesired canvas of chaos.

i have become a masterpiece of messiness.

~lacking boundaries

i fantasized about the end
only in heaven, if you are found
is it only exaggerated in my head?
i am tired of looking for you around

i do not feel worthy of your love
spilling my words of blasphemy
smothering my desire to rise above
i watched myself become my worst enemy

wrapped in the shaggy shroud
will you please cover all this pain?
dispersing into the black cloud
i wish to never be found again

how many times did i twist your soul
now that no one is left to blame?
collapsing into the placid sinkhole
i wish you never have to see me again

who shall i be in your absence?
the fear pulsated through my veins
how to not loathe my own existence?
i am the one binding myself in these chains

~ the real enemy

i wish i had more hours in a day
i would have filled them with your smile
i saw your vacant eyes turning away
you said, "it would only take a while"

i wish i had more rhymes for the fable
i would have prayed for you a little more
watching you leave the dining table
throwing plates, then cleaning the floor

i wish to have forgiven you sooner
and let you blame my eyes
all i remain now is a part of your humor
for seeing right through your lies

may you no longer have to conform
i now see you for who you are
your gentle rain turned to a perilous storm
and i drove straight in with my car

~ the crash

my head sinking into your chest
your shirt soaked with my tears
i said, "you have been my home
for the past three years"

between your smooth curves and rough edges
is where my body fits perfectly
i kept on holding onto us
but what made it so easy for you to leave?

she took everything she could
the swindler, who robbed me
she was wearing the brown hood
that i used to wear to sleep

maybe that home
will never be my home again
it turned into a shelter for a
shameless swindler in pain

my scent will linger
in all your sweet moments of affection
the mirrors of my home
will soon start to look for my reflection

~ because that's how i built it

time doesn't know how to mend
it only pushes you into a circle
with no beginning and no end
harrowed and starved in the eternal

out of false hunger
you start devouring your own tail
afraid of the sound of thunder
finding comfort on the bed of nail

again, and yet again
you find yourself at the starting line
the infinite is a game
where you forget you are divine

it's just the nature of the soul
it heals, it creates, it destructs
in order to again feel whole
it expands, it breaks, it corrupts

in the depth of deep darkness
you will find the brightest flame
there will be celebration of oneness
when you are tired of being the same

as the golden sun gleamed on my skin
a feather fell flowing from the skies
it takes me back to the park on that swing
with my brother and his caramel eyes

my long suffering chooses the next face
love, you have always made me greedy
so, watch me slip into a stranger's solace
as i watch everyone else walk ahead of me

is it the malediction of my femininity?
why do we decorate our superfluous ache
questioning all her bovine serendipity?
i sat weeping with my mother by the lake

in the slow summer bliss
i watched these leaves turn gray
i learned to comprehend every word
that silence has been yearning to say

~ the silent womanhood

throw mud over my clothes
and bricks of doubts over my existence
i will make a house instead

take away my pen and paper
snatch every alphabet from my mouth
my eyes will narrate the story instead

reading your words of revulsion
recalling the words filled with your disgust
i will write a poem instead

take away my book
i will write one instead
force me to bloom
i will be a cactus instead

pull my hair back mercilessly
ruthlessly and unapologetically
i will cut them short instead

drain my blood to quench your thirst
welcome your skepticism over my femininity
i will bleed to give birth instead

~ the voiced womanhood

on the cold ground as you lay
the dirt stuck on the sole of your feet
there lingers the scent of decay
this is where faith and fear meet

pulled recklessly under the quicksand
you smiled with no desire to be saved
these words only for you to understand
did i care so much that i misbehave?

you have given me enough
can you please give me some more?
there lingers the scent of love
i gave myself away only for you to ignore

i began to like the smell of dust
making friends with spiders and flies
the void of this never-ending distrust
makes me leave without saying goodbyes

amidst all the words said but not meant
i kept romanticized about my sad ending
caught up with the same old pretend
it is then your heart stopped intending

~ the forsaking

it sits on my chest
there's no face to this grief
this is where the violence rests
there is no sign of relief

it rips off my skin
i watch them run out of salt
it poked me with the sharpest pin
and i couldn't let myself revolt

it roars in my throat
like my words are no longer mine
the promises kept me afloat
and tears stirring inside my windpipe

it smashes my gut
you'll find nothing inside
my flesh is sore like an open cut
knowing you'll never be on my side

i will let you play your part
but you no longer can lead me astray
i will feel you in my heart
but i won't let you stay

it fractures my soul
defenseless to your attack
it turns me gold, turns me whole
the grief gently leaving through these cracks

~ the anxiety

where did our childhood go?
bright colors and the loamy fragrance
when did the ache turn to sorrow?
now we weigh everything in the balance

where did the butterflies go?
oh, my stomach is so empty within
when did the praise turn to echo?
now we are only playing to win

when did we shut our eyes
and watched our sisters suffer?
we turned deaf to their cries
and faithfully failed as a mother

when did we beget the bullies
and swallowed our own voices?
when did we wrap our injuries
and blamed the world for our choices?

the bullied became a bully himself
the daughters took after their father's rage
some were denied the cry for help
and only a few voices found the stage

where did this child go
the one who was full of love?
what did this child know
he was closest to the heaven above

how to make this heart melt
and soften it enough to mold into divine?
forget how the unfairness of the world felt
and make all your suffering mine

if i ever happen to feel your pain
there'll be no blind leading the blind
we will break free from the chain
oh, sacred surrender, just keep me kind

~ the bully

Poems of Gratitude

where did you come from, my damselfly?
i was alone, but now you're here
with the lights out, on my bed as i lie
unafraid, waking up to the morning prayer

i scared the fears away
they once feasted on my soul
"nothing can save you," they say
but remembering you made me whole

i showered with my eyes closed
for the first time i could
i am sure i was misdiagnosed
but now i finally feel understood

let the wall strike through my body
now nothing can break me
in the courtroom when they undrape me
you will save me like you saved Draupadi

did you save me from dying
by putting me through death again?
next to the lake where i found you smiling
you blessed me with the gift of pain

the pain rising from my spine
reminding me of the feelings i should have felt
when i was three, when i was nine
running in the garden, putting on my school belt

i pushed it back for so long
i don't know how to face it
i now know why it was wrong
staying when i should have quit

will i ever be loved?
i wonder lying in his bed
will i ever be enough?
i wonder as he kisses my forehead

this pain has taught me how to feel
is it a part of me that i couldn't kill?
at the counter, we had to turn around and leave
these empty pockets can't pay the hospital bill

the darkness of shadow
darkest when it was denied
and i kept weaving a moonbow
from all the tears that it cried

why did i become like this?
when exactly and how?
a distasteful denial on my lips
a pernicious pride refusing to bow

the world turned monochrome
and all the colors were taken away
like an orphan longing for a home
who eats leftovers from the crossway

in the sincerity of my art
i versified the words of violence
in the goodness of this heart
i found the secrets of silence

forgiving those who did me wrong
i freed myself by cutting down the string
the darkness dispersed into a song
and i bloomed like the first flower of spring

~ the blooming

she crawled into my arms
no, i didn't tell her about my day
like she understood everything
without me needing anything to say

she embraced me
with those tiny hands
the less i speak
the more she understands

she put her arms around me
while we slept on the floor
like she is telling me to rest
"i'm here, you won't be lonely anymore"

she is only six
but she is so wise
somehow, she knew
how to read between the lines

~ loving daughter

as i stood silently in the local train
she ran and clung tight to my knee
her mother chased her, but it was in vain
for she ran and hid behind me

have i always been this tall?
oh, i am no longer the one hiding
have i always headed for my fall
without knowing the fun of siding?

the dark, blameless eyes
play hide and seek
the fearless joy in her cries
rolling down her grimy cheek

shall i miss my train
or let her get caught?
should i turn her in
or save her a happy spot?

she was barefoot, covered in dirt
i untied my hair and lent her my favorite band
i must say, growing up didn't hurt
as her fingers reached for my hand

when i felt distant with myself
and my faith was crumbling
all my heavens turned to hell
misguided by my own suffering

when i couldn't find him
you reached out to me
through my win and my sin
you helped me to be me

your light guided me to see
i let all my shame evaporate
i fear that you see through me
but your love conquers my hate

i will forever be indebted
you turned my failures into lessons
all my demons were beheaded
by the sword of your lovely suggestions

~ true master

walking in your footsteps
i watched the sun going down
like the seashells lying at the beach
i find myself lost in the roaring crowd

they sink to the bottom
the shells that did not break
the broken ones lie here forgotten
looking through the smile they fake

like we took a trip to neptune
and atoms stopped spinning in their orbits
like we didn't care about our fortune
dance of the maidens in the glory of their wits

waiting for water to turn gold
the shells lie alone yet divine
all the broken pieces were pretty and bold
but no one cared if they were fine

she couldn't find her mother
this girl reminded me of myself
i told her we will find her together
the shells in our pockets are a big help

~ the seashells

under the depths of an estranged emotion
i let the silent waves crush my soul
drowning in a bottomless ocean
i saw a girl covered in charcoal

"how long have you been there?"
wrecked ships and dead fish around
her body filled with wounds of despair
i called her, but she didn't make a sound

some blood, some paint dissolved in water
her heart persistently refused to start
did she ignite all her charcoal and paper
only to light the fire of her art?

did you let someone steal your fire?
did you allow someone to make you ignore?
did you let someone else conspire?
then what's the universe here for?

the girl loved to draw faces
the faces she no longer recognized
the six strokes alignment and spaces
paintbrush yearning to be memorized

i checked her pulse, her breath
she didn't have much time
from the ocean of frame and death
i started singing my melancholic rhyme

it feels so heavy down below
only if i could carry you up above
i will just hold you and let us flow
take the charcoal and ignite my love

under the winter sun
she waits by the entrance
with patience of a nun
and a nonchalant remembrance

tangerine blossom of the widow's thrill
she slowly tilts the flowerpot
said, "sometimes it is okay to kill
before the roots begin to rot"

under the winter sun
she gives someone a new life
with patience of a nun
and the care of a wife

a hesitant grin with a gentle gaze
i ogle as she tucks her hair behind
her skin sparkles in the golden rays
but the mud on her forehead remains undermined

~ the gardener

the melancholy rolls down your eyes
and falls on my lifeless face
i lingered forever as your reprise
now watch me find my own grace

i am weeping your tears
you and i, shared the same womb
you held me close and covered my ears
when they yelled fighting in the next room

your selfless love aches my soul
counting clouds with my head on your lap
from eating in the same bowl
to fading slowly into a calm afternoon nap

back to the first guitar chord that you taught me
to all your stolen t-shirts that i have worn
let's go sometime and climb that mango tree
our innocence yearning to be reborn

~ dear brother

i have lived in different cities
new school uniform, new faces
what a heart that never pities
new walls, new places

i hate to leave it all behind
the screeching sound of the tape
what a heart that never pinned
new roads, old escape

to the new lanes of the unknown
i addressed my fond memories
learning about life on my own
new house, old centerpiece

as soon as it starts to feel familiar
i would have to let it all go
my sentience will always be inferior
holding out against the flow

it caused my soul to estrange
doesn't matter if i'm here or there
i know now why things have to change
and to embrace it, i cut my hair

i welcomed it with open arms
i rejoiced in its arrival
i learnt about its charms
and its necessity for survival

through the seasons i sit
from winters to summers
i no longer despise it
new life, new colors

~ the changes

i see the signs, i see the lights
covering my room
i feel the wind, it's late night
it's a full moon

when i'm defeated, just retreated
covered in the blood
when i'm not needed, only conceited
covered in the mud

when it's too late, the world is full of hate
when all the fairytales turn to tragic
i would still believe in your magic

i believed the words, followed the herd
who is myself?
i stood in the rain, talked with the birds
when there was no help

if i won't tell you what i am concealing
would you dare?
if i am hurting, more than healing
would you care?

when it's too late, the world is full of hate
when all the fairytales turn to tragic
i would still believe in my magic

as the golden sun blends in with my skin
i became more familiar with the roads
my heart, this is where you have been
come to me before this frame erodes

the cynicism of the landlord
lovers sobbing in separate rooms
the first cry, the first reward
an address to visit before their tombs

the bricks put together with trust
walls witnessing infidelity and despair
i saw the leaves flirt with the gust
then finally falling to tangle up in my hair

from one branch to another
i kept watching my nest break
from strangers to lovers
drawing chalk outline around my ache

it wasn't either about the space
the attic or the echoes in abyss
home was never a place
a person or a thing to miss

the temple in my chest and my sacred skin
the lyrical limbs and the scars yet to heal
my heart, this is where you should have been
a home free from the ordeal

~ the home

floating feathers of a dreamcatcher
at the window on my right
my life was stolen by a snatcher
so, i sing in the hands of death every night

the smell of my skin on this bedsheet
and the pillow soaked with tears
you will always live with the ghost of me
watch the tear-stained face fighting all the fears

the arms of the clock are still
like my arms that went cold
is it always about paying the bills
or the laundry that i will never fold?

the guitar doesn't sound well
and i have to leave the music behind
you tossed my heaven for the hell
yet the cassette played the memories in rewind

i pull my guitar closer to my heart
how can i not touch those strings?
i have to let go before it tears me apart
it's funny how we find home in simple things

Poems of Reflections

i will keep the windows of my room shut
i don't want more of you to come by
the violent storm led to the power cut
in this small room, you and i

tired of chasing the moonlight
you finally came and rested on my guitar
you must have put up a brave fight
yet, spiraling into fire left us both scared

around the candle, you danced all night
in the morning, you lie dead on the floor
i will wrap you in cloth just to be polite
let the waves wash you off the shore

we both danced around the light
hoping for some warmth near the fire
we both got blinded as it was too bright
sliding back into the shadows of our desire

~ mr. moth

the torn-off edges of your square
are you proud of what you've turned into?
how do you feel lying there all by yourself
letting people walk all over you?

do you also long to find your true colors
ashamed of the imprints they left?
are you too tired of pleasing others
or the feeling you shouldn't have felt?

they rubbed their feet clean
you took all their dirt
they defined your destiny
and you took all the hurt

would you be able to recognize yourself
the freshness and the shine?
or did you again offer the help
while they kept criticizing your design?

you absorbed all the stains
making all their filth yours
they hanged you through the rains
making all their guilt yours

you are deprived of love and care
wishing all of this wasn't true
how do you feel lying there
and letting people walk all over you?

cover me with decorative flowers
sit around for a few peaceful hours
put a fence around my peripheral land
water and pluck me with the same hand

but i am the dense greenwood
meditative, mysterious, and misunderstood
the origin and keeper of the life force
both the destroyer and the source

you pull out weed from the garden's roots
as my trees weigh down bearing the fruits
the garden is full of fragrance and chirping
but this forest smolders before flourishing

pebbles pavement over the freshly cut grass
this forest of mine doesn't guarantee a pass
while the garden was carefully curated
my forest remains untamed and uncultivated

you sit under the shade
watching the butterflies and the bees
i carry the jungle in my braid
i'm the varmint, i am the trees

is it her long hair
or the mole on her chin?
is it her round face
or her soft dewy skin?

is it her plum, pink lips
or her big brown eyes?
is it her smile
or her slim thighs?

is it her taste in music
or the way she speaks?
is it her strawberry lip gloss
or her rosy cheeks?

is it her kind words
or her tiny body?
is it her laugh lines
or the way she reminds you of me?

sinking my feet in the tepid water
i drown myself in disbelief
listening to the terms of a tactful talker
i hoped to find some relief

playing with the bubbles of memories
i felt the water like you touching me
conspiring against the contemporaries
i held my breath underneath

blowing up the candles around
i kept burning to keep us warm
fading into the echo of your sound
i could no longer cause you any harm

forbidding this love to prevail
i set all my fears free
floating to the brim as i exhale
i was no longer afraid to breathe

i washed off the betrayal from my skin
an enemy disguised as a friend
i silently sobbed behind an insincere grin
and put this elusive love to an end

what if, the paper boats
never made it to the other side

what if, my heart melts
and dissolve into nothingness
before finding you

you wake up tired from the nap
feeling like you are not yourself anymore
he mocks you for wrongly reading the map
you could either fight or politely ignore

he likes his girl skinny
honey, i know you would starve
he likes his girl pretty
you wonder which piece of your body to carve

you wear that lipstick
the one that you got from your own money
his idea of love is so unrealistic
making you second guess your own worth, honey

and you wonder if you'll ever be enough
you watch him staring at other women
honey, it's a cage that you call love
fall from the throne and get stuck in the kitchen

cut your hair, dye them red
reclaim the power, reclaim the space
listen to your heart, and to your head
quit this chase and just win the race

you keep your dreams second
he keeps his needs first
there's no fixing in the backend
this love of yours is coerced

break free from the trap
soar as high as a bird
wake up from the nap
it's time to win the world

i walk back home in search of
long-lost comfort in a mother's lap
i push the prosaic elevator button
when all i want is to fall off the gap

i look for the keys in the wallet
i'm glad i put your picture in here
look in the mirror as i switch the faucet
do you recognize me, my reflection?

are you still there?

is this mine, the moment that begins at nine?
is this life, i wonder when the clock moves past five

a sigh of relief
the dreamers abandoned their dreams
"don't be no one and everyone"
the unfulfilled desire silently screams

who brought upon this frantic fear
leaving you alone buried into the dirt?
your blood and sweat is merely a souvenir
to decorate your chaotic cage of comfort

~ i walk back home to say goodbye

i count the flying airplane
sitting in this beguiling balcony
tangerine sky, please keep me sane
if you can't take away my agony

i haven't moved in days
only to watch strangers stroll the street
on this bed where my body stays
swiftly sinking, slowly embracing grief

i observe the shadows at play
with tall buildings within my sight
the nights morph into day
and the days dissolve into night

woe of a mother, reckless reasoning of a recluse
oh death and decay, dethrone my muse

i'll board one of these planes
before city lights blind my soul
your voice keeps me sane
mother, i'll soon be home

in the woods, don't you dare to chase her
watch the wolf rise in the eyes of a doe
at the dawn before she ceases into vapor
she found her nook in the afterglow

she wondered what it's like to have a choice
when she picked up the coin by the lake
the loud silence again shunned her voice
one side was love and the other was rage

the dragonflies came to weigh her soul
circling around her whenever she dances
she knew she is only going to be whole
only when she is going to take chances

she washed her hands again and again
rubbed her lips till they bled
the sin lingers in the subtle waves of pain
and in between the lines that you've never read

the queen of serpents rose from the abyss
and the grace of healing grinding her to death
the dragonflies were not afraid of the hiss
gently feeding her so she could again catch her breath

she could only remember herself running
then one day she paused to look at why
the footsteps of someone coming
were louder than her helpless cry

the dark descended upon her
one day she finally opened her eyes
the sun did turn her into vapor
and she was a firm believer of goodbyes

the newborn dragonfly got colors in her wing
dweller of deep hells turning to light
i saw her getting off the ground and swing
unarmed, the warrior won the fight

~ the dragonfly

the food used to taste better when i was a child.
i yearn for the aroma of freshly cooked rice
wafting through the air as I step off the school bus.

I long for the anticipation of lunchtime
eagerly waiting to unwrap the love
packed in my lunchbox.

i wonder why the food doesn't taste the same anymore.

i have a cook now
and there's no one waiting by the rice cooker
for it to cool down.

sitting in a dark room
i patiently waited for my end
who will put flowers on my tomb
when i couldn't even keep a friend?

these needles and syringes
hurt less than a betrayal
death is away only a few inches
busy painting a sorrowful portrayal

the poison reached my veins
before love could make its way
i looked at the shadows on the curtains
as the internal wounds start to decay

i am too exhausted to pray
i guess, i am not at all brave
i feel sorry for pushing everyone away
i wonder if you'll decorate white lilies on my grave

my hair clogging the drain
and my bones feel lonely and tired
my last wish is to drench myself in the rain
will you miss the real me or the version you admired?

i looked out of my window
the sidewalk and the breeze
we kissed under the lamppost
i can picture it perfectly

these nights are always harsh
they force me to wonder about
the year, the month, the day, the hour, the minute, the second
when love left us

we started speaking less
and screaming more
we started adoring less
and abusing more

we started loving less
and fucking more
we started accepting less
and blaming more

we kiss less
we lie more
we smile less
we laugh more

the person i used to like,
i can't find him in 'you' anymore

the nights are always cold
they keep me wondering about
the year, the month, the day, the hour, the minute, the second
when love left us

is it okay if we don't talk for a few days?
is it okay if i choose to stay away?

let's just not talk for a few days!
let's just let each other go away!

it is okay to not talk at all.
it is okay for me to get away.

~ stages of departing

what will happen when -
a jasmine falls in love with a sunflower?

one blooms at night,
the other can't live without the sun.

what will happen when -
a dreamer falls in love with a pragmatist?

one lives under the inked sheets,
the other operates on utility.

what will happen when -
contradiction falls in love with confirmation?

one speaks soft and slow,
the other hears the shadow screaming.

what will happen when -
my scars make love to your scar?

heaven to hurricane,
i wonder which one you are?

Bonus Section
(I)

The Shadow: Overlooked Rhymes

i have made friends with silence
i have made peace with violence
spoken twice, got beaten thrice
living in a hell that you call paradise

if nothing here belongs to me
don't look at me with anticipation
in a world full of greed
i am starving for your affection

you have tried to fit expectations
on this body and soul like a glove
in a world filled with abomination
i am famished for your love

i forgot the sound of my voice
gave me options but never a choice
wanted the world for me when i could be the one
you have enticed the moon wanting to be your sun

i wore a blue dress on my 16th birthday

gathering all my courage
i wore it once again

imitating your hands as i started unzipping the side chain

i'm not sure if i was stuck in the past
or just finding excuses to cling to your memories

in a constant tussle with 16-year-old me
who wasn't ready to let you go

i found you all over me—
from the v-neck to the frill of the dress
and still, i wasn't over you, yet

but i decided to take away your rights
you can't hurt me anymore
i cut down all the strings
and calling off this puppet show

i no longer want to be like you
i will be more like me
so, i wore that dress again
paired them with my favorite heels

it was no longer for you
it was only for me

"i'll write about you when this all comes to an end," i gasped
"what will you write about?" he smirked.

"that it would have been better if
we met a little earlier or a little later
it would have been better if
we had not met at all

the way you swipe my hair off my face
with your nose when i won't let go of your hands

the way you used to pause after saying my name
i wonder why you never complete your sentences
but i think i do now.

you wanted to check if i was still around
after you stab me with your condescending words
after you feast on my soul's flesh

the way you shamelessly admit that
you will never play songs for me when i go away"

"umm, will you sing for me when i am gone?"
i asked with anticipation.

"no, i guess i will not,"
he responded without hesitation.

~ delusional love

(you will only see what i want you to see)

the girl with pretty brown eyes
ogling over for your attention
but i see you desperately searching
for love in my eyes

were you spellbound or cursed?

don't you know that
i am a magician
and you are another card in the deck
for my sleight-hand trick?

(you will only see what i want you to see)

the girl in the skimpy outfit
throwing herself over you
but i see your eyes piercingly touching
every inch of my skin

did my convincers leave you spellbound?

i do not want to lose the mechanical grip
this gimmick has no secret doors
either you go on living
or you get cut into two halves

boy, who will save you from yourself?
how will you break the spell?
don't you know you aren't allowed to leave
once you have arrived at my magical hell

~ welcome to my magic show

hello…
i have a complaint

you probably think i'm insane
and wonder why my glass is always half empty
i will fill it with my complaints
as i've always been too scared to see

i will point out the points you miss
then smother you with your insecurities
wounds to rub salt over, wounds to kiss
i see you are already tired of my impurities
hello…
i have one more complaint

no, do not mistake me for a crybaby
don't smother me with your affection
i know you will hit me with a hot ladle
when i reveal all my imperfections

i will let this loathing curl my toes
i can't deny, i love how it feels
i love thorns, how dare you bring me a rose
i will rupture your heart before it heals

hello, i have a...

i tried to memorize the art of brewing our morning coffee
one for me, one for you.

two teaspoons of sugar
half teaspoon of coffee
1/4th glass filled with hot milk
pour some cold milk to the brim

i remember how your eyes used to glisten
as you stirred the spoon in the glass
i remember the milk on your mustache
across the corners of your pretty grin

i start reminiscing about the time when we used to have
breakfast together

the abnegation
felt like amnesia
'cause i can't remember now
what your coffee used to taste like

the taste was abating like the flavor of our youth

i imitated the movements of your hands
watched the sugar dissolving in the milk
the syrupy coffee was appetizing but noxious
a bittersweet metaphor for our love

i wish i could tell you
how worthless memorizing the steps were

i have tried 243 times now
my coffee never tasted the same
i can't seem to find the secret ingredient
was it your love or mine?

i wish i could tell you,
i drink tea now.

i am surfeited with deafening silence
all the words of comfort
remind me of merciless violence

the voices in my head told me
the clock stays still in this paradigm
sinking endlessly in a sorrowful sea
"what day is it, what time?"

my body covered in dirt and flies
and no flower blooms here
the sun doesn't set, the sun doesn't rise
and i no longer care

demons turn their back on me
after feasting on my blood and meat
demons turn their back and sleep
leaving me in the cold to weep

the walls of this room are closing in
and these windows turned into an alibi
voices told me if i want them to stop
then either one of us has to die

come lie with me in silence
embrace me with the dirtiest grip
sedate me in your essence
align me with the magnetic dip

melt my bones under the skin
pour your acid on me
blow out the lights within
give me the third degree

i will blow my plucked eyelashes
was my truth too appalling?
i will burn myself in your ashes
as you got tired of my stonewalling

you and i are one
aggrieved and love-deprived
i would rather face it than run
better late than to never have arrived

~ the overt abuse

the tears rolled back in the eyes
but my soul cried to belong
will i succeed after the thousand failed tries
or would this agony linger lifelong?

there's no one who could listen
the sadness in the joyous melody
my melancholy will make their eyes glisten
and the sad ballads will only be a parody

i too shall be sacrificed, in the end
the side dish at supper
it was hosted by someone named friend
the love let down on my upper

my throat is dry and the lips are glued
i'm the least preferred dish at the barbecue
they put their forks & spit me half chewed
my fervor twisted, grilled and served to you

the spiral of galaxies in my womb
weeping for the lives i couldn't give birth to
all my fetus devoured and consumed
and i was made to catch sight of the view

~ the misunderstood artist

sensing him in every lover
in every man
i keep revisiting my pain

like my body is not loved
but is being defiled
over and over again

slide the silk robe off my shoulder
grab my hair in your fist
this is the last time before i get older
will you show me why i exist?

stay when the love leaves
from my neck, untie your albatross
i wish you'd bring hell upon me
before heaven is born out of chaos

i want you to hear the silence
as you glare at me for a while
explain to me the difference between
making love and getting defiled

i want you to see me beyond the lies
that you might have heard from others
slide those red lace off my thighs
take me in as sand devours the sea waters

this is the last time
i will be twenty-two tomorrow
you can see me smile, but
when will you learn about my sorrow?

oh, he was a demon playing god
who promised me heaven

he likes girls with backstories
finding peace in their agony
he gives them a shoulder to lean on
feeding his masculinity

he likes girls with issues
feeding his pride and ego
he only gives to take it all away
finding comfort in their miseries

"you are one of them—
a miserable, anxious little poet"
"it's time to make love to you
there's endless pleasure in your sorrow"

his heaven was my misery
oh! he was a demon playing god

whenever our eyes meet, will you please not let them revolt?
those eyes, for sure, have some stories that need to be told

i wish i didn't know about the wart behind your left ear
i can't and i shouldn't touch you, for us to stay in the clear

she has beautiful long hair, big wide eyes
she smells like you every morning, with her mouth full of lies

i want to have you before she accuses
i want to touch you without these excuses

every time i see you biting your lower lip
the devil robs the heart out of my rib

if you ever wonder how to solve this riddle
i'll be waiting around lust and lies
or somewhere in the middle

escaping your game
i long to look into your eyes
i have spelled your name
in the stars of the clear skies

it hasn't rained in weeks
i can't see the flowers die this soon
and my heart keeps wondering
if you still have the tie that i gave you

how do you face yourself
after everything you have put me through?
i have started to realize
it never meant anything to you

you said, "it always rains on my birthday"

i want to tell the tales
of how you burn people alive
and it hasn't rained in weeks
but yes, it rained on 25th of July

i will lose my veil
and let you pour despair
let them safely return from the sail
then i may let you untangle my hair

oh, i'm scared
should i open my window and let you in?
oh, don't you dare
turning into a cuckoo and reliving your sin

your wrath is insufferable
i cover my ears with my hand
i am tired of hiding under the table
heaven is yours but this is my land

your screeching voice pierces my chest
i will swim in your tears, falling from the sky
let the birds fly back to their nest
oh, my storm, would you please calmly pass by?

~ the storm

oh, sweet pleasure to my pain
please help me let go of my last breath
i walk crying and screaming in the rain
like a widow waiting for her death

please put an end to my suffering
the storm has passed but you haven't embraced me yet
how to pay back for my mother's nurturing?
oh, my father, i am forever indebted to your sweat

instead of lighting diyas on your safe return
i should've burnt the whole town instead
you just left, leaving me here to yearn
all my past lives decorated in your bed

i walked on fire for your sake
but you were nowhere to be found
your crown adorned with my ache
now watch me return to the ground

he says he doesn't like his crooked-teeth grin
(i love it)
he says he doesn't like the tan on his skin
(i love it)

he is the master of geography
so i will be his planet
he is the master of diplomacy
so i will be his cabinet

he plays dirty
he plays clean
he knows how to get me alone
on the stairway to nicotine

i carry the serenity of lakes
he carries the virtues of temples
he loves me rough
but his love is gentle

i worry about the trying times
he always talks about the silver lining
does he know 800.673 miles
leaves my heart pining?

he loves Beatles
a fan of the Queen
i love how he gets me alone
on the stairway to nicotine

~ 800.673 miles

i remember hitting the right side of my head
we were too sober to keep control
that's when you decided to keep your hand
between my head and the subway pole

you dropped me off at home
why did you kiss my forehead thrice?
i would be too sad if i couldn't recall
any of this after the sunrise

i will choose to fall and get hurt
but only a fool assumes before trying
if you say you didn't feel a thing
i know you would be lying

you told me to stay away from you
i can't help but wonder why
recalling how you whispered half-heartedly
"you should rather be with a good guy"

the wind in your long hair
enticed my desires with lust
the gap between your thighs
has always gotten my thirst

all above or down below
i will quietly run my fingers
say "please" or scream "no"
i'll jolt as long as your scent lingers

look how you are living your dreams
gotten all used to my cruelty
i would love to hear your muffled screams
when i gag you with your panty

the only black magic i know
lingers on your upper lips
you are now in drowning water
does it feel good on those tips?

so pure, so dirty
let me leave you haunted
your smile tells me
this is all you ever wanted

and don't let go of the eye contact
i know how to make you go crazy
i will love you the way you've always wanted
this is the time you submit to your lady

you smell like perfume and cigarettes
boy, you reminded me of someone i still regret—

yes! bad and handsome, he was

just throw a mean fuck and do as you please
i won't ask you to stop till you make a mess out of me

don't ask me my name; i don't really care about yours
you can search for her in me; i will search for my cures

i won't mind if you imagine pulling her hair
digging into her hips
you'll know when i imagine touching his face
kissing those lips

yes! rough and deep, his voice

just throw a mean fuck and keep me in your favorite view
i won't ask you to stop till you make my body black and blue

i will ask you to wear your clothes and leave
i am a woman you can only dream of, but you can't keep

a mother sat with her child
beneath the plumeria tree
an innocence that is undefiled
my adolescence longs to be as carefree

i witnessed the creation as a midwife
then strangled it to death
i wonder how this kid is full of life
and i'm wishing for my last breath

i recall the hands of my mother
i hate to see them getting older
not sure if i'll ever be a good daughter
but she can rest her head on my shoulder

i romanticize about the end
this joy of living is bittersweet
the sweet agony of separation descends
everything i loved will eventually leave

rebellion to the decree
the unending quest for power
i walked down that plumeria tree
and crushed the plumeria flower

i lied to protect you from hurt
but you no longer trust me
no number of apologies will be enough
i am left with no options but to leave

in this cruel world
i thought you would be by my side
too naive to notice
i have nowhere to hide

i want to lay my head in your lap
and cry till my eyes melt like my belief
i will then go jump off the gap
hoping to give myself some relief

i will keep this note
behind our family photograph
or i will make a paper boat
from every poem draft

i am sorry for the times i made you cry
i am sorry for all the pain i put you through
i will love you till my veins run dry
but i might never be able to tell how much i loved you

~ suicide note

you gave me a piggyback ride
when i had my shin fractured
you helped me walk up the stairs
you helped me walk down the slope

but you had destroyed me with the same hands
that used to carry the weight of my bag

you hit me unforgivingly
'cause i couldn't save you a seat in the bus
the no-show at the hospital concludes
that the love has finally left us

i walk up the stairs now
controlling my urge to jump off the railings
i walk down the slope now

i continued doing everything you did to me
i am just doing it without you

~ abusive relationships

Bonus Section (II)

The Mirror:
Lonely Meditation

i saw my reflection in you

i was thrilled and scared at the same time
thinking about the potential i carry to
nurture and destroy

the mirror doesn't reveal the truth
it reflects what you desire to see

~ what's your truth?

i'm grateful i wrote that letter to you before your fever broke
seeking forgiveness and cherishing our memories together

the night you passed away, a part of me died too
but i find solace in knowing that you knew—
i loved you
that i was mistaken
and that you were
and will always be
my best friend

~ letters to Adya

your voice silences the thoughts
that keep running in my head
my fingers need not make a cross
moments of weakness, we are infrared

like the first ray of the sun
fell on the cold barren ground
one more rule and i'm done
will you look for me when i'm not around?

tell me, what are you reading?
tell me, what goes inside that messy head?
tell me the reason why you started writing
moments of weakness, we are infrared

through the dark, we found each other
your smile being my biggest help
can i just pull myself out of this mirror?
have you met someone just like yourself?

at times
i feel your pain more deeply than you do

sometimes
i suffer in your suffering more than you do

almost always
i love you more than you do

~ the attachment

melancholy fuels my heart and
sadness becomes my canvas

i have always thought of myself as an artist
but i don't know who am i without my sorrow

for how long are you going to lie to yourself
- saying it doesn't matter when it churns inside of your gut

for how long you are going to lie to yourself
- if it didn't matter, you wouldn't have been here

~ tactful liar

you hurt me for the things that i did
you hurt me more for the things that i did not do

was it all accounted for?

~ conditional love

i was rooting for you to touch the sky
and you rooted me out of the ground
i started to decay
and you took the next morning flight

~ the indifference

i often read notes to self in your voice

my depression wasn't a handicap
it was as if some feelings tiptoed through my veins
refusing to leave until my limbs fell off

when i was longing for love, my heart always felt so empty
now when i am pouring my love out
my heart feels like an incessant river

there are only two ways to undermine women:
by belittling their achievements
and questioning their character

today is the last day,
last hour,
last minute,
last moment
i think of you

(13:21, 02/02/2024)

~ unfulfilled desires

pain brings us closer together, while suffering unites us

~ evil serves a purpose

i love the intricacies of human nature—
sometimes serving as medicine
other times as mirrors

oh! i found myself falling in love with a stranger who was reading next to me on a train

secretly, i've never felt good enough

so i put on my finest attire
and complain about the world
for seeing me
for who i truly am

~ the imposter

i don't understand love if it doesn't utterly destroy me
i don't merely want to fall in love
i want to be engulfed by it

i sometimes ponder the purpose behind creation
i wonder if it's the universe making love to itself

perfectly, it carries the imperfections
bravely, it embraces the dark side

silently, it controls the tide
swiftly, it survives all the phases

gently, it embraces all the scars
flawlessly, it accepts all its flaws

persistently, it fights the shadows to become whole again

~ i envy moon

i am crying in a cafe
i am crying in a stranger's car
i am crying on the lonely bed
i am crying in the shower
i am crying in the cab
i am crying in my sleep

i think it's time you hold me down
i dare not cry in the arms of death tonight

~ end this suffering

hug this book if you felt understood